DATE DUE

HOLIDAY ORIGAMI

Valentine's Day Origami

by Ruth Owen

PowerKiDS
press™

New York

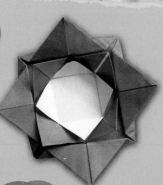

Published in 2013 by The Rosen Publishing Group, Inc.
29 East 21st Street, New York, NY 10010

Produced for Rosen by Ruby Tuesday Books Ltd
Editor for Ruby Tuesday Books Ltd: Mark J. Sachner
US Editor: Sara Antill
Designer: Emma Randall

Photo Credits:
Cover, 1, 3, 5, 7, 8 (bottom), 12, 17 (top right), 20 (left), 21 (top right), 24, 29 (top right) © Shutterstock.
Origami models © Ruby Tuesday Books Ltd.

Library of Congress Cataloging-in-Publication Data

Owen, Ruth, 1967–
Valentine's Day origami / by Ruth Owen.
    p. cm. — (Holiday origami)
  Includes index.
  ISBN 978-1-4488-7865-9 (library binding) — ISBN 978-1-4488-7924-3 (pbk.) — ISBN 978-1-4488-7930-4 (6-pack)
  1. Origami—Juvenile literature. 2. Valentine decorations—Juvenile literature. I. Title.
  TT870.O957 2013
  736'.982—dc23
                          2012009647

Manufactured in the United States of America

CPSIA Compliance Information: Batch # B4S12PK: For Further Information contact Rosen Publishing, New York, New York at 1-800-237-9932

Contents

Origami in Action	4
Get Folding!	6
Be My Valentine!	8
Origami Two-Color Hearts	12
Origami I Love You Message	16
Red Rose Valentine's Greeting	20
Swan Heart Boat	24
Friendship Bracelets	28
Glossary, Index, Websites	32

Origami in Action

Origami is the art of folding paper to make small models. Working with just a single sheet of square paper, you can make a bird, a bracelet, or even a red rose. You don't need glue or scissors. It's all about making the right folds and creases!

Origami gets its name from the Japanese words "ori," which means "folding," and "kami," which means "paper." This art form has been popular in Japan for centuries.

Inside this book you will find step-by-step instructions for making a range of origami models for Valentine's Day. You can make your models using colorful origami paper or use scraps of gift-wrapping paper. You can even use pages from old magazines.

All you need to do is get folding and creasing, and you'll soon be hooked!

Get Folding!

Before you get started on your Valentine's origami models, here are some tips.

Tip 1

Read all the instructions carefully and look at the pictures. Make sure you understand what's required before you begin a fold. Don't rush, but be patient. Work slowly and carefully.

Tip 2

Folding a piece of paper sounds easy, but it can be tricky to get neat, accurate folds. The more you practice, the easier it becomes.

Tip 3

If an instruction says "crease," make the crease as flat as possible. The flatter the creases, the better the model. You can make a sharp crease by running a plastic ruler along the edge of the paper.

Tip 4

Sometimes, at first, your models may look a little crumpled. Don't give up! The more models you make, the better you will get at folding and creasing.

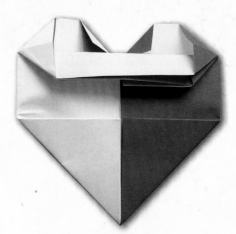

When it comes to origami, practice makes perfect!

In this book, you will get the chance to make a red rose and a swan for Valentine's Day. The flowers and swan on this page were made by experienced origami model makers. Keep practicing and maybe one day you will be an origami master!

This flower model is called a *kusudama*. It is made from lots of individual models that are then glued or threaded together to form a ball. Kusudamas are made in Japan as decorations or to be given as gifts.

Check out this fun origami heart made from a dollar bill. Money origami is a popular offshoot of origami. It's also a fun and creative way to give someone a gift of cash!

Be My Valentine!

No one knows for sure how Valentine's Day became a day to show and celebrate love. February 14, St. Valentine's Day, was the feast day of a Christian **saint**, St. Valentine, who was executed by an emperor of ancient Rome because he would not give up his Christian beliefs.

In 1382, an English poet, Geoffrey Chaucer, called St. Valentine's Day the "day when every bird cometh ... to choose his mate." In the centuries that followed, February 14 became a day when people showed their love by sending romantic greetings and giving gifts.

You can get started on your Valentine's Day preparations with this easy to make origami heart.

To make origami hearts, you will need:

Sheets of origami paper in red, pink, or purple

(Origami paper is sometimes colored on both sides or white on one side.)

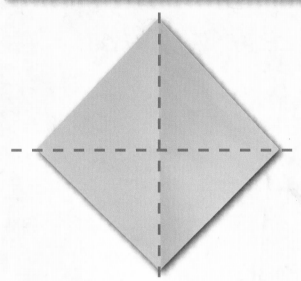

STEP 1:
Place the paper colored side down. Fold along the dotted lines and crease.

STEP 2:
Fold down the top point to meet the center and crease.

STEP 3:
Fold up the bottom point to meet the top of the model, and crease.

STEP 4:

Fold in the right side along the dotted line so it lines up with the center of the model, and crease.

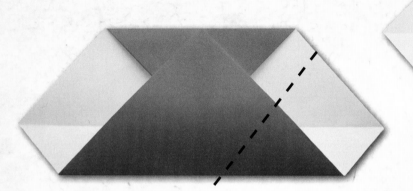

STEP 5:

Now fold the left side into the center so the two sides meet, and crease.

STEP 6:

Turn the model over and fold in points A and B. Crease well.

A   B

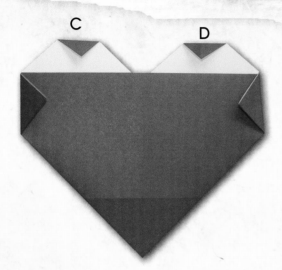

STEP 7:
Now fold down points C and D, and crease well.

STEP 8:
Turn the model over and your origami heart is complete!

STEP 9:
Make lots of hearts in red, pink, and purple to create Valentine's decorations, or to decorate handmade Valentine's Day cards.

Origami Two-Color Hearts

When you think of Valentine's Day, you probably think of red hearts. In ancient times, doctors, scientists, and poets alike thought of the heart as the center of human emotions, including love.

Today, of course, we know that our hearts don't make us fall in love. We also know that the familiar round, symmetrical heart shape looks nothing like a real human heart. The heart, however, is still used worldwide as a **symbol** of love and romance.

Today, hearts appear on T-shirts, bumper stickers, boxes of candy, and Valentine's cards. No matter what language you speak, if someone sends you a heart, you know it means love!

To make origami two-color hearts, you will need:

Sheets of origami paper in red or your favorite colors

(Origami paper is sometimes colored on both sides or white on one side.)

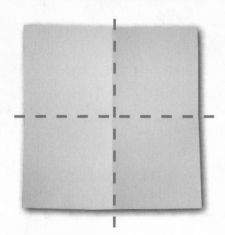

STEP 1:
Place the paper colored side down.
Fold along the dotted lines and crease.

STEP 2:
Now fold the left side into the center and crease.

STEP 3:
Fold the bottom half back behind the model, and crease.

STEP 4:
Fold the right side into the center and crease.

13

STEP 5:

Now turn the model over. It should look like this.

STEP 6:

Fold the two top corners back behind the model, and crease well.

STEP 7:

Unfold the folds you've just made on the top corners. Fold down the top of the model and crease well.

STEP 8:

Now open up the paper in the fold you've just made and squash flat along the top of the model.

STEP 9:
Now fold down points A and B, and crease.

STEP 10:
Now fold up the two bottom corners to meet in the center, and crease well.

STEP 11:
Turn the model over and your two-color heart is complete. This model looks great half white and half colored, or use origami paper that has a different color on each side.

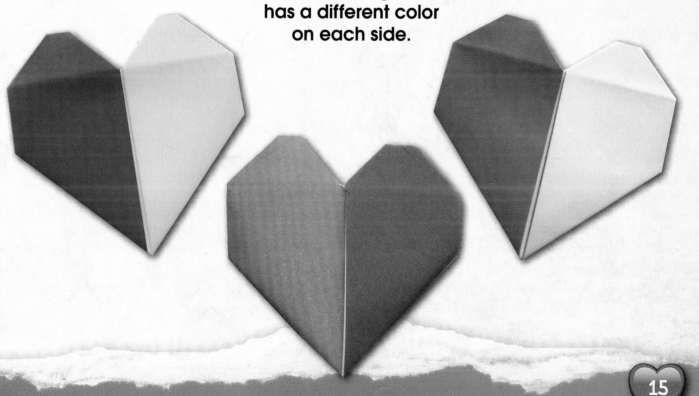

Origami I Love You Message

What we call valentines have been around for centuries. One of the earliest is a note sent by an English duke to his wife while he was imprisoned around 1415. Today his valentine is in the British Museum, in London. Over time, valentines were manufactured and decorated with hand-painted pictures and lace. Handwritten notes gave way to mass-produced printed cards, and today, thanks to the Internet, we can send "e-cards" to those we love.

This year make a personalized "I Love You" origami Valentine's message for someone you love. You will need to follow the instructions here, and make the heart on page 8.

To make an origami Valentine's message, you will need:

3 sheets of origami paper

If you are using 6 x 6 inch (15 x 15 cm) origami paper, a piece of craft or construction paper approximately 12 x 7 inches (30 x 18 cm)

Glue

(Origami paper is sometimes colored on both sides or white on one side.)

STEP 1:
To make the letter "I," place the paper colored side down. Fold along the dotted lines, and crease.

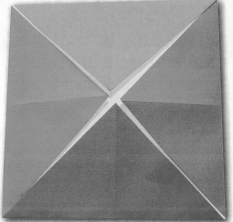

STEP 2:
Now fold the four corners into the center, and crease.

STEP 3:
Now fold in two sides so they meet in the center, and crease.

STEP 4:
Turn the model over, and your letter "I" is complete.

STEP 5:
To make the letter "U," take another piece of paper and repeat steps 1 and 2.

STEP 6:
Now unfold the four creases, flatten the paper, fold in the two sides, and crease.

STEP 7:
Fold up the bottom point, and crease.

STEP 8:
Fold the top point along the dotted line behind the model and crease.

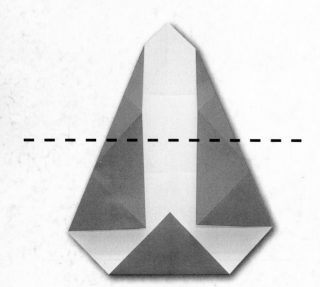

STEP 9:
Fold in the two sides of the model and crease.

STEP 10:
Turn the model over and fold point A behind itself along the dotted line, and crease.

STEP 11:
Your letter "U" is now complete.

STEP 12:
Now glue your letters and heart to the craft paper. Your Valentine's message is ready!

Red Rose Valentine's Greeting

Roses have long had the power to stir feelings of passion. The ancient Greeks and Romans were among the first to create a connection between roses and love. The rose was a **sacred** sign of their goddess of love, named Aphrodite in Greece and Venus in Rome.

Wild red roses came to Europe from China in the 1800s. Plant experts combined those red roses with other kinds to create the rich red roses we know today.

Follow these steps to create your own perfect combination of color and emotions—a valentine in the form of a beautiful red rose!

Be my Valentine!

To make the red rose greeting, you will need:

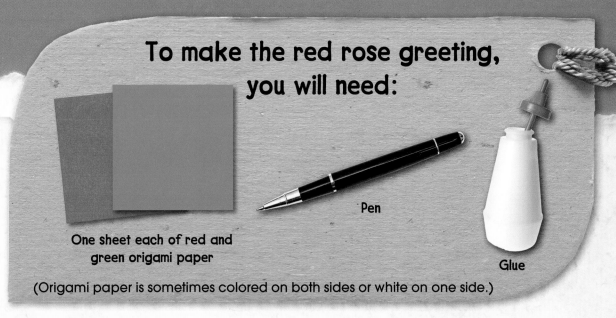

One sheet each of red and green origami paper

Pen

Glue

(Origami paper is sometimes colored on both sides or white on one side.)

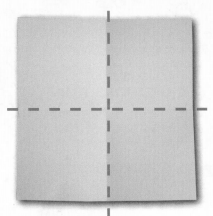

Be my Valentine!

STEP 2:
In the center of the paper write a short Valentine's message. The message can only fill about 1 square inch (2.5 cm²) of paper.

STEP 1:
Place the paper colored side down. Fold along the dotted lines, and crease.

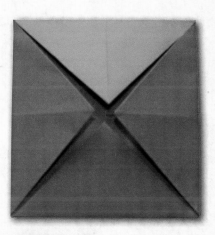

STEP 3:
Now fold the four corners of the paper into the center and crease.

STEP 4:
Fold the four corners into the center of the model again, and crease well.

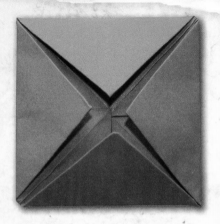

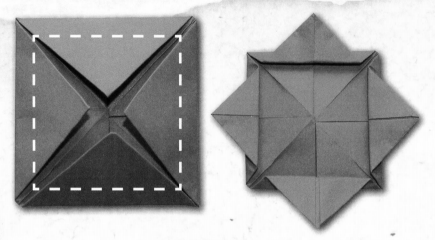

STEP 5:

Now fold the model's four corners into the center for a final time. The paper will be very thick, so crease hard.

STEP 6:

Fold the four top flaps of the model back along the dotted lines, and crease well.

STEP 7:

Now fold the next four flaps inside the model back on themselves, and crease.

STEP 8:

Finally, fold the last four flaps in the center of the model back on themselves, and crease. Your message will now be revealed!

STEP 9:

To make the leaves, place the green paper colored side down. Fold it in half diagonally, and crease. Then fold one half of the triangle into the center, and crease.

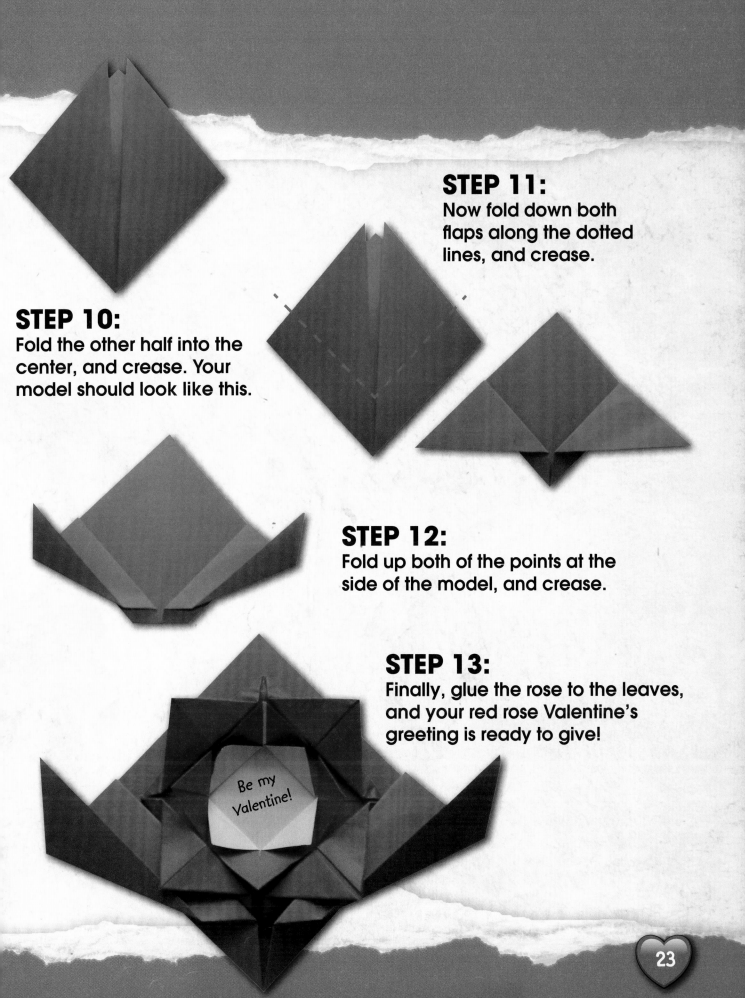

STEP 10:
Fold the other half into the center, and crease. Your model should look like this.

STEP 11:
Now fold down both flaps along the dotted lines, and crease.

STEP 12:
Fold up both of the points at the side of the model, and crease.

STEP 13:
Finally, glue the rose to the leaves, and your red rose Valentine's greeting is ready to give!

Be my Valentine!

Swan Heart Boat

A pair of beautiful white swans is an image often associated with love and romance. No one knows, however, why these large water birds are considered romantic. It could be because swans often find a mate and then the pair stays together for life!

To make the swan heart boat, you will need to follow the instructions here and make the heart model on page 8. Your swan heart boat can be used as a decoration. You can even write a message on the heart and have a beautiful origami swan deliver your Valentine's greeting!

To make a swan heart boat, you will need:

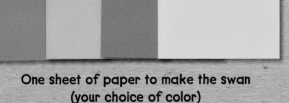

One sheet of paper to make the swan
(your choice of color)

One sheet of pink or red
paper to make the heart

(Origami paper is sometimes colored on both sides or white on one side.)

STEP 1:

Place the piece of paper for the swan colored side down. Fold the paper in half diagonally and crease. Then open up the fold you've just made.

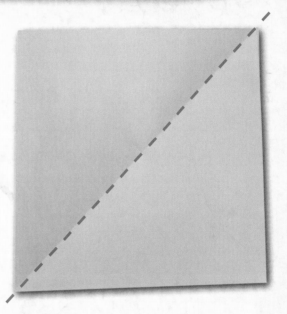

STEP 2:

Fold both sides of the paper into the center and crease.

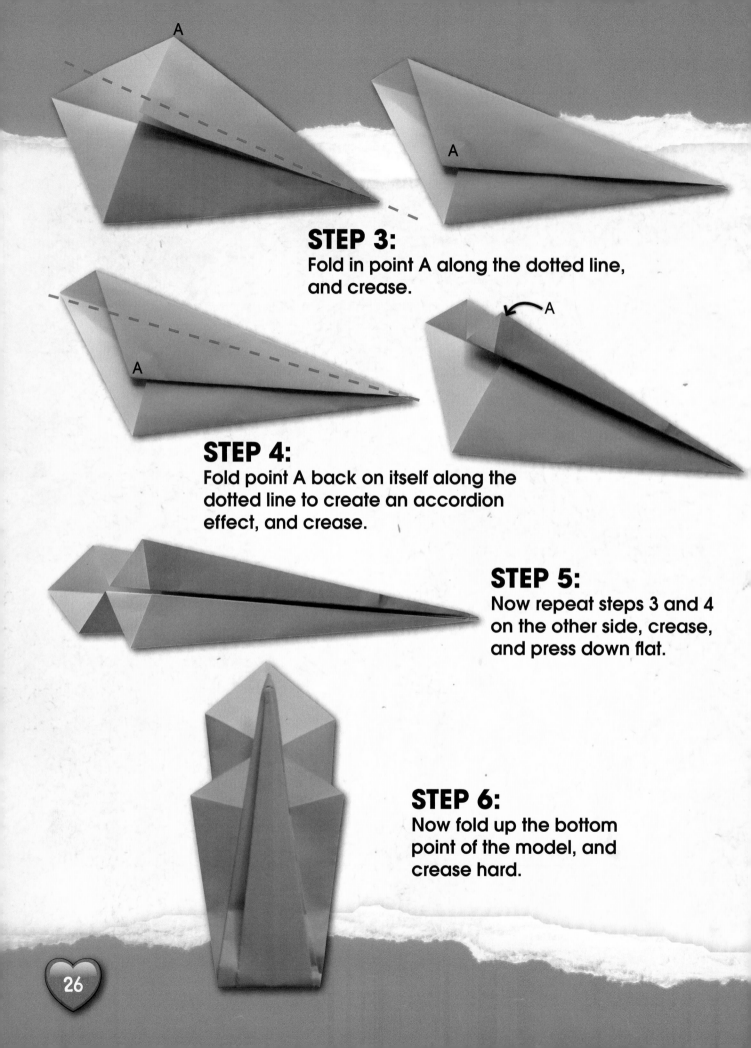

STEP 3:
Fold in point A along the dotted line, and crease.

STEP 4:
Fold point A back on itself along the dotted line to create an accordion effect, and crease.

STEP 5:
Now repeat steps 3 and 4 on the other side, crease, and press down flat.

STEP 6:
Now fold up the bottom point of the model, and crease hard.

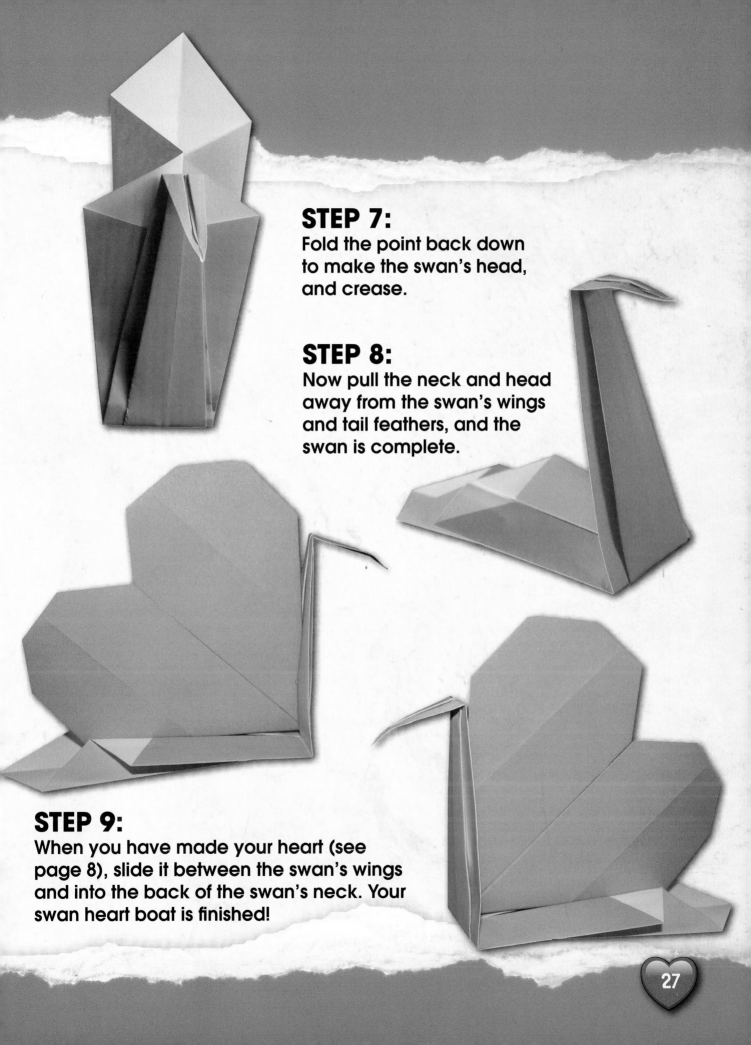

STEP 7:

Fold the point back down to make the swan's head, and crease.

STEP 8:

Now pull the neck and head away from the swan's wings and tail feathers, and the swan is complete.

STEP 9:

When you have made your heart (see page 8), slide it between the swan's wings and into the back of the swan's neck. Your swan heart boat is finished!

Friendship Bracelets

Friendship bracelets are worn as a symbol of a strong friendship between two people. It is **traditional** for one friend to make a bracelet then give it to another. The idea is that the maker has spent time and effort creating something to show how much he or she cares about the friendship. Sometimes friends make a matching pair of bracelets and wear one each.

Friendship bracelets are usually made from colorful woven thread and beads, but it's possible to make them using origami, too! This project shows you how to make a brightly colored origami friendship bracelet to give to a special friend this Valentine's Day.

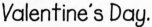

To make friendship bracelets, you will need:

Sheets of origami paper in your favorite colors

Tape

(Origami paper is sometimes colored on both sides or white on one side.)

STEP 1:

Place the paper colored side down. Fold the paper in half diagonally, and crease.

STEP 2:

Unfold the paper. Now fold in half diagonally again, but this time fold so that the edges of the paper don't quite meet up and the white side of the paper is showing. Crease well.

STEP 3:

Now fold up the bottom edge of the triangle, and crease. The fold should be about .5 inch (1 cm) deep.

STEP 4:

Turn the model over and fold up the bottom edge again. Use the previous fold as a guide for how deep to make the fold. Turn the model back over and it should look like this. You can see the bracelet's pattern appearing.

STEP 5:

Keep turning and folding up the bottom edge of the model.

STEP 6:

When the whole triangle of paper has been folded, your model will look like this. If you still have a small point of paper in the center, tuck this behind your last fold.

STEP 7:

Wrap a thin strip of clear tape around the center of the bracelet to hold the folds together. When you are ready to put the bracelet on or give it to a friend, gently shape it into a circle, slide the two ends into each other, and use tape to secure them.

STEP 8:

Make bracelets for your best friends this Valentine's Day to show them how important their friendship is to you!

Glossary

origami (or-uh-GAH-mee) The art of folding paper into decorative shapes or objects.

sacred (SAY-kred) Something that is very important because of its connection to a religion or to a god or religious person, such as a saint.

saint (SAYNT) A person recognized for his or her good deeds and holy nature, usually by a Christian religion.

symbol (SIM-bul) Something that stands for or represents another thing, such as an important event or person. A cross may be a symbol of Christianity.

traditional (truh-DIH-shun-al) Something that has been a custom, belief, or practice for a long time and has been passed on from one generation to the next.

Index

A
Aphrodite, 20

F
friendship bracelets, 28
friendship bracelet origami
model, 28–31

H
heart origami model, 8–11
hearts, 8, 12

J
Japan, 4, 7

K
kusudamas, 7

L
love, 8, 12, 20, 24

M
money origami, 7

O
origami, 4

R
roses, 4, 7, 20

S
Saint Valentine, 8
swan heart boat origami model,
24–27
swans, 7, 24

T
two-color heart origami model,
12–15

V
Valentine's cards, 12, 16
Valentine's Day, 4, 7, 8, 12, 28
Venus, 20

Websites